The JESUS PRAYER
A Gift from the Fathers

By Father David Hester

CONCILIAR PRESS
Ben Lomond, California

Printed in Canada

THE JESUS PRAYER:
A Gift from the Fathers
© Copyright 2001 by David Hester

Published by   Conciliar Press
                 P.O. Box 76
                 Ben Lomond, California 95005-0076

ISBN 1-888212-26-8

About the author:
The Very Rev. Father David Hester is pastor of St. Mary Antiochian
Orthodox Church of Wilkes Barre, Pennsylvania. He earned his Masters
degree from the Graduate Theological Union in Berkeley, California,
and his licentiate and doctoral degrees in oriental ecclesiastical studies
from the Pontifical Oriental Institute in Rome, Italy. He is married to
Dr. Anne Hester.

CONTENTS

"**L**ord Jesus Christ, Son of God, have mercy on me." These few simple words, known as the Jesus Prayer, are of great importance to the Christian East—so much so that they are often called the summation of all Orthodox spirituality. The nineteenth-century writer, Bishop Ignatius Brianchaninov, wrote of this prayer:

> Examine all the Holy Scriptures: You will find the Name of the Lord exalted and glorified everywhere in them. . . . Study the writings of the Fathers and you will see that all of them, without exception, suggest and advise the practice of the Jesus Prayer. . . . Finally, turn to the canonical decrees of the Eastern Orthodox Church and you will find that . . . the Church has established the recitation of the Jesus Prayer as a substitute for the reading of psalms and prayers in one's own cell or room.[1]

This prayer, used by so many men and women of the Christian East, reflects so well the heart of Eastern Christian spirituality that its use is recommended for both the beginner and the proficient as the driving force in their life of prayer.

In this brief work, the principal area of attention will be how this prayer comes to us from the earliest days of the Fathers to our own time. It is hoped that this little prayer, which comes to us as a great gift and opportunity, will begin to resound within us, and we will come to pray it not only often, but at every moment of our lives.

A word which will appear frequently throughout this work, with which some readers may be unfamiliar, is *hesychasm*. *Hesychasm* stems from the Greek word *hesychia,* which entered into the vocabulary of Christian spirituality in the fourth century. It has become a technical term to designate the state of inner rest and silence, gained through victory over the passions, which allows one to proceed to contemplation.

Hesychasm refers to the Orthodox spirituality that attains the perfection of the person by union with God through perpetual prayer. Its greatest characteristic is its precise affirmation of the excellence and necessity of *hesychia,* quiet, to attain this union.

Hesychast spirituality emphasizes inner recollection and private, continuous prayer, practiced in solitude and silence. It particularly values the practice of the Jesus Prayer, in the many different forms of its development, as one of the chief means of attaining both outer and inner quiet. It is in the milieu of the hesychasts that the Jesus Prayer developed, from the time of the fourth-century desert monks onward.

THE EARLY CENTURIES

One group within the Eastern Christian Church has, throughout history, continually exerted a great influence on the entire Church—those in the monastic life. From the time of Saint Anthony in the third century, hermits, monks, and monasteries commanded the reverence and respect of all Christian people and exerted a particularly strong influence on the spirit of Eastern Christianity. The Church adopted the monastics' liturgy, their spiritual way, and their type of holiness.

In fact, it is from well-respected monastic communities that certain practices and emphases gradually converged to form the Jesus Prayer as we know it. Two of these factors are of primary importance: the practice of frequent repetition of short prayers, and the great respect in which the Name of Jesus was held.

The early Church had received from the Sacred Scriptures a strong respect for the Divine Name. There are many references in both Testaments to the respect in which God's Name was to be held. An Eastern monk, writing on the significance of the Divine Name, writes of the Old Testament:

> If the divine name is invoked upon a country or a person, it belongs henceforth to Yahweh; it becomes strictly his and enters into intimate relations with him (Gn. 48:16; Dt. 28:10; Am. 9:12). The name abides in the temple (3 Kgs. 11:3). The name is a guide in man's life and in his service of God (Mi. 4:5). Throughout the Psalms, the divine name appears as a refuge, an auxiliary power, an object of worship.[2]

In the New Testament too, the same significance is given to the Name of Jesus, particularly in the Book of the Acts of the Apostles:

> It is above all, the Acts of the Apostles which could be called the book of Jesus. "In the name of Jesus" the good news is preached, converts believe, baptism is conferred, cures and other "signs" are accomplished, lives are risked and given.[3]

Among the desert monks themselves, there are many references to the power of the Name of Jesus. There are accounts of exorcisms performed by using the Name of Jesus, and a number of the *Apothegmata* (Sayings of the Desert Fathers) deal with the Name of Jesus.

But even more significant for the later growth of the Jesus Prayer was the early development in the desert of monological (one-word) or short-phrase prayers. The Desert Fathers gave great prominence to the ideal of continual prayer, insisting that the monk must always practice what was termed "secret meditation" or "the remembrance of God." To help in this task of perpetual recollection, monks took some short formula which they repeated over and over again. For example, we find "Lord help," "Lord, the Son of God, have mercy upon me," or "I have sinned as a man, do Thou as God have mercy."

In this early desert period there was a great variety of these short prayers. It took several centuries before these prayers were combined with the invocation of the Name to form the Jesus Prayer.

Saint Makarios of Egypt and His Disciple Evagrios
Among the early teachers of the desert, there are two who had an abiding influence on Orthodox spirituality, especially on the growth of the Jesus

Prayer. These are Evagrios of Pontus (346–399) and Pseudo-Makarios, whose writings were thought to be those of Saint Makarios. (The real Saint Makarios of Egypt, c. 300–c. 390, was Evagrios' master in the desert.) The influences of the two, however, were very different. Evagrios applied Neoplatonism, with its emphasis on the mind, to the desert spirituality, while Pseudo-Makarios, with a more biblical outlook, emphasized the totality of the person, represented in the heart.

There are very few of the real Makarios' own works still in existence; however, in these few, he appears as one of the first teachers of a short prayer which had as an essential element the Name of God, Lord.

> They asked Abba Makarios, "How should one pray?" The old man answered: "There is no need at all to make long discourses: it is enough to stretch out one's hands and say, 'Lord, as you will and as you know, have mercy.' And, if the conflict grows fiercer, say: 'Lord, help me!' He knows very well what we need and shows us His mercy."[4]

Most of Saint Makarios' influence on later spirituality is in fact not really his own, but rather that of an unknown author of the fifth century who wrote the *Fifty Spiritual Homilies* that came down under the assumed authorship of Saint Makarios. In these homilies, Pseudo-Makarios strongly emphasizes the biblical union of mind and heart, of body and soul. He shows us that the whole man, body and soul, must be reintegrated through asceticism and purification, so as to gain self-control and be able to live in constant awareness of the presence of God.

Pseudo-Makarios' teaching has its basis in the Incarnation. Prayer is not aimed at freeing the spirit from the impediment of the flesh. Since the whole person, body and soul, was created in the image of God, the whole person is called to divine glory. In his fifteenth homily, Pseudo-Makarios writes:

> It is like this in Christianity for anyone who tastes the grace of God: "Taste and see how sweet the Lord is." Such a taste is this power of the Spirit working to effect full certainty in faith which operates in the heart . . . His very grace writes in their hearts the laws of the spirit. . . . For the heart directs and governs all the other organs of the body. And when grace pastures the heart it rules over all the

members and the thoughts. For there, in the heart, the mind abides as well as all the thoughts of the soul and all its hopes. This is how grace penetrates throughout all parts of the body.[5]

Pseudo-Makarios' understanding of the heart and of the union among body, mind, and soul was to have a great influence in the later development of the theology of the Jesus Prayer.

To better appreciate the significance of Pseudo-Makarios' teaching on the heart, we must compare his understanding to that of the disciple of Makarios, Evagrios Pontikos. Evagrios too has had a strong influence on Eastern Christian spirituality. In fact, down through the centuries, a tension has existed between the understandings of these two men in Eastern Christian thought.

Evagrios was the first intellectual to adopt the life of the anchorites in the Egyptian desert. He not only took on their ascetic practices and their life of prayer, he also tried to integrate their outlook into the philosophical system inspired by Neoplatonism. Evagrios was a disciple of Origen, and he used the Neoplatonic principle of dualism as the basis for his doctrine of prayer.

According to this principle, the spiritual and the material worlds were looked upon as completely separate and alien to each other. The spiritual world, the realm of the soul and mind, was considered to be important and the material world, the realm of the body and of matter, was considered to be a prison and the enemy of the spiritual. Anything that took form from the material world was considered to be a hindrance in prayer. This principle is seen especially in two of Evagrios' works, the *Praktikos* and the *Chapters on Prayer.*

The heart of Evagrios' teachings on prayer can be found in the following quotes from his *Chapters on Prayer:*

9. Stand resolute, fully intent on your prayer. Pay no heed to the concerns and thoughts that might arise the while.
11. Strive to render your mind deaf and dumb at the time of prayer and then you will be able to pray.
66. When you are praying, do not fancy the Divinity like some image formed within yourself. Avoid also allowing your mind to be impressed with the seal of some particular shape,

but rather, free from all matter, draw near the immaterial Being and you will attain to understanding.

110. Keep your eyes lowered while you are praying. Deny your flesh and your desires and live according to the mind.[6]

Evagrios accents the intellect in prayer and has only a few scattered references to the Word and Trinity, and no reference to the Incarnation, the Church, or the sacraments. He conceives of prayer as an immaterial contact of the intellect with God.

Evagrios' teaching was posthumously condemned, along with that of Origen, at the fifth Ecumenical Council in 533. His writings, however, continued to be recopied and disseminated by being attributed to Saint Neilos. In fact, Evagrios' teaching continued, in spite of his condemnation, to be very influential. In the sixth century Saint John Klimakos, while opposing him on certain points of doctrine, called him the "Messenger of God." Saint Maximos the Confessor in the same century criticized Evagrios severely, even while incorporating most of Evagrios' ascetic doctrine into his own work.

By far, Evagrios' most enduring contribution was in his formation of expressions and vocabulary to describe the desert spirituality. His vocabulary continued to be used down through the centuries, and gradually there was a marriage between the Evagrian and Makarian understandings. Evagrios' spiritual notions were subjected to a Christological corrective, and the Evagrian mind and the Makarian heart were united as the "mind in the heart."

This is particularly true for the authors Diadochos of Photike and John Klimakos, who synthesized Evagrios and Makarios so that, as John Meyendorff writes, the " 'intellectual prayer' of Evagrios became in the East the 'prayer of the heart,' a personal prayer explicitly addressed to the Incarnate Word, the 'Jesus Prayer' in which the 'recollection of the Name' holds essential place."[7]

Also during the fourth century, there are two other early references to the primitive Jesus Prayer. Saint Basil the Great in the thirty-seventh part of his *Great Rule* for monastic life states that each monk must practice "perpetual prayer." Saint John Cassian, in his *Collationes*, written on the spirituality of the desert monks, describes at length the perpetual invocations used by monks in the desert.

Saint Diadochos of Photike

In the mid-fifth century, Saint Diadochos, the Bishop of Photike of Epeiros, was one of the greatest popularizers of desert spirituality in the Byzantine world. In his *One Hundred Chapters on Perfection,* he recommends purification of the heart by calling to mind the "memory of Jesus." In Chapter 85 he writes:

> Grace at first conceals its presence in those who have been baptized, waiting to see which way the soul inclines; but when the whole man has turned towards the Lord, it then reveals to the heart its presence there with a feeling which words cannot express. . . . If, then, a man begins to make progress in keeping the commandments and calls ceaselessly upon the Lord Jesus, the fire of God's grace spreads even to the heart's more outward organs of perception, consciously burning up the tares in the field of the soul.[8]

Saint Diadochos speaks of closing the mind and filling it with Christ:

> When we have blocked all its outlets by means of the remembrance of God, the intellect requires of us imperatively some task which will satisfy its need for activity. For the complete fulfilment of its purpose we should give it nothing but the prayer "Lord Jesus." [9]

Thus Saint Diadochos is the first writer to refer explicitly to the remembrance of the Name of Jesus, even though he does not offer any exact form for the invocation.

It is, in fact, sometime in the sixth or seventh century that the full text of the Jesus Prayer is first found. This is in the *Life of Abba Philemon,* an Egyptian hermit. Philemon was once asked by a younger monk what he should do to keep his mind from being distracted.

> The Elder replied, "Keep watch in your heart; and with watchfulness say in your mind with awe and trembling: 'Lord Jesus Christ, have mercy upon me.' For this is the advice which the blessed Diadochos gave to beginners." [10]

Later, when this same brother, John, returned for further instruction, he was told:

Without interruption, whether asleep or awake, eating, drinking, or in company, let your heart inwardly and mentally at times be meditating on the psalms, at other times be repeating the prayer, "Lord Jesus Christ, Son of God, have mercy upon me."[11]

Thus from the sixth century on, this living tradition of the Jesus Prayer has continued uninterrupted within the Orthodox Church.

Growth at Mount Sinai: Saint John Klimakos

In 527 Justinian I established at Mount Sinai the famous monastery of Saint Katherine, an event and place that was to have great influence on the future of the Jesus Prayer and hesychasm. The most outstanding of all the spiritual teachers of Mount Sinai was the monk John (570–649), an abbot of Saint Katherine's Monastery. John was given the name Klimakos due to the work that made him famous: *The Ladder* [*Klimax* in Greek] *of Divine Ascent.*

The Ladder is a detailed presentation of monastic spirituality in thirty steps. Its focal point is the invocation of the Name of Jesus. Saint John frequently uses Evagrian vocabulary; however, he strongly acknowledges the place of the body in prayer. In fact, some of his texts can lead one to believe that he already knew the practice of uniting the Jesus Prayer to breathing, a practice adopted by later hesychasts.

In the following few texts we will see the heart of his teachings on prayer:

In your prayers there is no need for high-flown words, for it is the simple and unsophisticated babblings of children that have more often won the heart of the Father in heaven. Try not to talk excessively in your prayer, in case your mind is distracted by the search for words. One word from the publican sufficed to placate God, and a single utterance saved the thief. Talkative prayer frequently distracts the mind and deludes it, whereas brevity (*monologia*) makes for concentration. (Step 28)

Close the door of your cell to your body, the door of your tongue to talk, and the gate within to evil spirits. . . . It is better to live poor and obedient than to be a solitary who has no control over his thoughts. . . . Stillness is worshiping God unceasingly and waiting on Him. . . . Let the remembrance of Jesus be present with your every breath. Then indeed you will appreciate the value of stillness. (Step 27) [12]

Saint John does not offer any definite formula in his recommended use of monologic prayer; however, he does unite this prayer to the constant memory of Jesus' Name. In Saint John there is found an anticipation of future hesychast theories which were developed particularly in the fourteenth century.

Following the writings of Klimakos, the most important writing to come from Mount Sinai on the use of the Jesus Prayer was *On Watchfulness and Prayer*, by Pseudo-Hesychios. This work was at first erroneously attributed to Saint Hesychios, a mid-fifth-century priest from Jerusalem. It was written, however, definitely after Klimakos, since it quotes Saint John's passage: "May the name of Jesus be united to your breathing." This work is probably a compilation from several authors who had some connection with the monastery of Vathos on Sinai.

In Pseudo-Hesychios we find this passage:

> Truly blessed is the man whose mind and heart are as closely attached to the Jesus Prayer and to the ceaseless invocation of His name as air to the body or flame to the wax. The sun rising over the earth creates the daylight; and the venerable and holy name of the Lord Jesus, shining continually in the mind, gives birth to countless intellections radiant as the sun. [13]

This is the first time that the expression "prayer of Jesus" appeared. It is also the first time that there is such a clear connection of the prayer with breathing, as is seen in another paragraph of the work, where "ceaselessly breathing Jesus Christ" is recommended as a constant daily activity.

Saint Maximos the Confessor

Living at the same time as Saint John Klimakos, although not a member of the Sinai monasteries, was Saint Maximos the Confessor, another monk who was to exert a great influence on the understanding of the place of the Jesus Prayer in hesychasm. Saint Maximos was part of the line of Eastern Christian mystics, following Saint Gregory of Nyssa, who sought to express the fundamental realities of Christian spirituality in the framework of Neoplatonic philosophy.

Maximos used the principal elements of the mysticism of Saint Gregory of Nyssa, especially his Christology and his doctrine of deification (the gradual process by which a person is renewed and unified so completely with God that he becomes by grace what God is by nature). Saint Maximos describes the deified state as a "total participation in Jesus Christ." He writes:

> The admirable Paul denied his own existence and did not know whether he possessed a life of his own: "I live no more, for Christ lives in me" (Galatians 2:20). . . . [Man], the image of God, becomes God by deification; he rejoices to the full in abandoning all that is his by nature . . . because the grace of the Spirit triumphs in him and because manifestly God alone is acting in him; thus God and those worthy of God possess in all things one and the same energy, or rather, this common energy is the energy of God alone, since he communicates himself wholly to those who are wholly worthy.[14]

For Saint Maximos, salvation consists in being conformed totally and freely to the divine energy or will. This understanding of the aim of the Christian life as the union of wills was to influence greatly the development of the hesychast tradition in its valuing of unceasing prayer as the way to accomplish this union.

Saint Symeon the New Theologian

There are no known outstanding texts dating from the eighth and ninth centuries relative to the Jesus Prayer. It is known that the prayer existed, that its practice continued, and that it already formed a part of the Byzantine spiritual tradition. Its form, however, was fluid, with the Name of Jesus being the most important element.

It is in the teaching of Saint Symeon the New Theologian (949–1022), a monk of the Studion Monastery and later Abbot of Saint Mamas in Constantinople, that the theology of hesychasm was further developed. Saint Symeon is one of the greatest names in the history of Orthodox spirituality. Unlike most other Byzantine ascetic and mystical writers, he wrote in a style which spoke of his own personal encounter with God. There are two strong emphases in his writings: the primacy of spiritual experience, and the reality of Christocentric mysticism.

Jaroslav Pelikan, a twentieth-century historian, writes of Saint Symeon's spirituality:

> The true monk was one whose dedication to Christ enabled him, by divine grace, to acquire a mystical awareness of the divine presence. . . . Or as Simeon said in one of his hymns, not only had the believers become members of Christ, but Christ had become their member as well: . . . "Christ is my hand and Christ is my foot . . . and I am the hand of Christ and the foot of Christ."[15]

Saint Symeon himself received mystical experiences of Christ, as he relates:

> Though Thou thus didst often silently appear to me, hidden so that I could not see Thee at all, yet I saw Thy lightning flashes and the brightness of Thy countenance, as aforetime in the waters. Again and again they encompassed me, but I was unable to seize hold of them; so I was mindful of how I had seen Thee on high. . . . Thou who are invisible to all, beyond thought or comprehension, didst appear to me, and it seemed to me as though Thou wast cleansing my mind and increasing its vision, permitting me to see Thy glory even more. It was as if Thou Thyself didst grow and shine yet more brightly. . . . Thou didst seem to me to come forth and shine more brightly, and didst grant me to see the outline of Thy form beyond shape. At that time Thou tookest me out of the world. . . . When I said, "O Master, who art Thou?" then, for the first time Thou didst grant me, the prodigal, to hear Thy voice. . . . Thou saidest, "I am God who have become man for your sake. Because you have sought me with all your soul, behold, from now on you will be My brother, My fellow heir, and My friend."[16]

Indeed, this experience of Symeon is the prime example of the religious experience desired by all hesychasts.

In Saint Symeon's writings there is no direct reference to the Jesus Prayer. It is known, however, that he used monological prayer. Saint Symeon's biographer, Nicetas Stethatos, writes of his life:

> At that time he was filled during prayer with great joy and suffused with burning tears. . . . Not yet initiated in such revelations, in his

amazement he would cry out without growing weary: "Lord, have mercy on me." . . . Finally, much later, when this light gradually withdrew, he found himself again in his body and inside his cell, he felt his heart filled with an indescribable joy, while his mouth cried aloud, as has been said: "Lord, have mercy on me."[17]

It is not clear whether this prayer is directed to Jesus or not, but it would seem so, since as was noted in the previous text, the voice that Saint Symeon heard in his vision stated: "I am the God who became man for love of you."

THE FLOWERING ON MOUNT ATHOS

It is the fourteenth century, the Golden Age of hesychasm, that is the high point in the development of the Jesus Prayer. In fact, over the following five centuries, there were three periods of great intensity in the practice of the prayer: the fourteenth century in Byzantium, the eighteenth century in Greece, and the nineteenth century in Russia.

In the thirteenth and fourteenth centuries there are four outstanding figures who greatly influenced the development of the Jesus Prayer: Saint Gregory of Sinai, Saint Nikephoros the Hesychast, Saint Theoleptos, Archbishop of Philadelphia, and above all, Saint Gregory Palamas, Archbishop of Thessalonica.

Saint Gregory of Sinai

Saint Gregory of Sinai (1255–1346) represents the end of the Sinaite phase and the beginning of the Athonite phase in the history of the Jesus Prayer. He was a monk from Sinai who, while living in Crete, learned of the Jesus Prayer from a monk named Arsenios. He later went to Mount Athos, where he found only three monks who were experts in the contemplative life. Saint Gregory instructed the monks there in prayer. From that point on, Athos gave its own particular stamp to the Jesus Prayer, as noted in *The Prayer of Jesus:*

> On Athos the prayer lost its first fluidity. But by degrees Athos established it firmly in a formula and it insisted oddly enough on the concomitant, psychophysical technique. In short, Athos exhibited greater rigidity.[18]

Saint Gregory's influence extended far beyond Athos. From 1325 on, the

Athonite eremitical monks, living outside the protective rampart of the great monasteries, were victims of Turkish attacks. So Saint Gregory left Athos and finally settled in Paroria on the border of Bulgaria, where he was protected by the Bulgarian Czar. From Saint Gregory's instruction there, hesychasm spread throughout the Slavic countries, where it reached a high point in the fifteenth-century movement of Transvolgan hesychasm under Saint Nil Sorsky (1433–1508).

The writings of Saint Gregory have always been very popular among Orthodox monks. He was imbued with the precepts of the *Ladder* and presented prayer with a deep understanding of the psychology of monks.

In his treatise, *On Contemplative Life and Prayer,* he sets down the theological foundations of the mystical life in this way:

> Even if we have been reborn in the Spirit our faith is dead and inactive. . . . There are two ways of finding the activity (energy) of the Spirit that was received sacramentally in Holy Baptism:
>
> (a) By the observance of the commandments and at the price of long efforts, we may achieve in a general way a revelation of this gift. . . .
>
> (b) It is revealed in a life of obedience to a spiritual father, by the methodic and continual calling upon the Lord Jesus, that is, by the remembrance of God.
>
> The first way is longer, the second is very short, provided that the soul has learned to dig the ground courageously and perseveringly in search of the hidden gold.[19]

The Jesus Prayer is seen as the indispensable aid to this growth in contemplation. In fact, Saint Gregory advises that a person pray in this way: One should remain seated and make a profound bow, pronouncing the formula, "Lord Jesus Christ, have mercy on me," with perseverance. This is done to bring about the union of the mind and heart which the hesychasts insist is essential for contemplation.

Saint Nikephoros the Hesychast

Another important Athonite monk of the fourteenth century is Saint Nikephoros the Hesychast (c. 1300). Saint Gregory Palamas said he was an Italian who converted to Orthodoxy and became a monk of Mount

Athos. Saint Nikephoros wrote the little treatise, *On Guarding the Heart,* and also *The Method of Holy Prayer and Attention,* which was at first falsely attributed to Saint Symeon the New Theologian.

In these works Saint Nikephoros unites ideas from many earlier monastic authors. From Saint John Klimakos he takes the idea of "linking the Name of Jesus to the breath"; from the *Spiritual Homilies* of Pseudo-Makarios, he takes the understanding of the body, soul, and spirit as a single organism, which sin alone breaks up; from Saint Symeon the New Theologian, he uses the idea that Christ came to reestablish unity within a person and that when one constantly recalls the Name of Jesus, the grace of redemption lives within.

Saint Nikephoros presents these elements as a series of spiritual exercises and counsels. In *On Guarding the Heart,* he presents excerpts from various writers and concludes with a discussion on attention. This conclusion is of great importance, because in it Saint Nikephoros points out what he considers to be the heart of hesychasm. He stresses that really to learn prayer, or to deal with any spiritual difficulties, a person needs an experienced spiritual father. The spiritual father is at the heart of hesychasm, for he is the only one who can instruct properly. (Frequently the practical details of the hesychast method are not clearly written out; it is rather assumed that a person will have a knowledgeable teacher to follow.)

Saint Nikephoros, however, does deal with the practical side of hesychasm; in fact, he concretizes for the first time the practices of hesychasm, which are often called the psychophysical method. At the end of *On Guarding the Heart,* he writes:

That is why we should search for an unerring guide, so that under his instruction we may learn how to deal with the shortcomings and exaggerations suggested to us by the devil whenever we deviate left or right from the axis of attentiveness. . . . If, however, no guide is to be found, you must renounce worldly attachments, call on God with a contrite spirit and with tears, and do what I tell you.

You know that what we breathe is air. When we exhale it, it is for the heart's sake, for the heat is the source of life and warmth for the body. The heart draws towards itself the air inhaled when breathing, so that by discharging some of its heat when the air is exhaled it may maintain an even temperature. . . .

Seat yourself, then, concentrate your intellect, and lead it into the respiratory passage through which your breath passes into your heart. Put pressure on your intellect and compel it to descend with your inhaled breath into your heart. . . .

Therefore, brother, train your intellect not to leave your heart quickly, for at first it is strongly disinclined to remain constrained and circumscribed in this way. But once it becomes accustomed to remaining there, it can no longer bear to be outside the heart. For the kingdom of heaven is within us (cf. Luke 17:21); and when the intellect concentrates its attention in the heart and through pure prayer searches there for the kingdom of heaven, all external things become abominable and hateful to it. . . .

Moreover, when your intellect is firmly established in your heart, it must not remain there silent and idle; it should constantly repeat and meditate on the prayer, "Lord Jesus Christ, Son of God, have mercy on me," and should never stop doing this. For this prayer protects the intellect from distraction, renders it impregnable to diabolic attacks, and every day increases its love and desire for God. . . .

Banish, then, all thoughts from this faculty—and you can do this if you want to—and in their place put the prayer, "Lord Jesus Christ, Son of God, have mercy on me," and compel yourself to repeat this prayer ceaselessly. If you continue to do this for some time, it will assuredly open for you the entrance to your heart in the way we have explained, and as we ourselves know from experience.[20]

Saint Nikephoros made very concrete and precise the role that Pseudo-Makarios had already assigned to the heart in prayer. He viewed the heart as the center of the person. It is around this center that each person exists as an indivisible psychophysical unity. It is in the depths of this unity that a person is to pray the Jesus Prayer.

In the *Method* there is even a clearer description of the psychophysical method. Unfortunately, that description is so clear that later translations of the work replace the passage with a footnote, for fear that it would lead the reader astray unless he or she learned it directly from a master. There is, however, a description of this passage in *The Prayer of Jesus:*

And now here is the central passage of the work. In order to pray, one must close the door of one's cell, place oneself in a state of quiet, sit down, press one's chin against the chest, look towards the middle of the stomach, restrain one's breathing, make a mental effort to find the "heart's source," while repeating "the epiclesis of Jesus Christ." At the beginning, one experiences only difficulty and obscurity, but soon one notices a kind of light. Henceforth, as soon as an evil thought arises, and even before it appears and takes form, it is expelled and destroyed.[21]

Thus, Saint Nikephoros closely connects the Jesus Prayer to various breathing and posture techniques. These techniques were later to be a source of controversy, and were eventually, especially in the nineteenth century, to be separated from the Jesus Prayer as unnecessary for praying the prayer fruitfully.

Saint Theoleptos of Philadelphia

The next important figure in the fourteenth century is Saint Theoleptos, Archbishop of Philadelphia (d. 1320). He was a married man and father, who, after the death of his wife, entered a monastery on Mount Athos and became a disciple of Saint Nikephoros. He is considered to be one of the greatest theoreticians of hesychasm, especially on its psychology. He analyzed the functions of the mind and applied to each of them a specific role in the practice of the Jesus Prayer.

Saint Theoleptos' analysis, according to the psychology of his day, connects the mind's functions to the Jesus Prayer in this way:

• The *dianoia,* the responsive process of logical understanding, conceives and repeats incessantly the Name of Jesus;

• the *nous,* the power of the intellect, intuits the truth directly;

• the *pneuma,* the spirit, creates love and sorrow for sin.

The function of the Jesus Prayer is to unite these three and focus them totally on the Trinity.

Saint Theoleptos became one of the chief inspirers of the renewal of hesychasm, introducing into it a strong emphasis on the sacramental and ecclesial aspects of spirituality. Saint Theoleptos, as Bishop of Philadelphia, was not in a cloister, nor in a desert, but rather closely linked to fourteenth-century social and spiritual reforms in Byzantine society.

Throughout his whole career he sought to encourage an ecclesial community and a sacramental spirit.

The importance of Saint Theoleptos, however, was overshadowed by that of one of his pupils whom he initiated into hesychasm: Saint Gregory Palamas (1296–1359), who became the theologian *par excellence* of hesychasm.

Saint Gregory Palamas, Defender of Hesychasm

Saint Gregory Palamas grew up in the court of Emperor Andronicus II Paleologos, his father being a member of the Byzantine senate. Andronicus was one of the most religious of the late Byzantine rulers. Gregory's father himself was so religious that he prayed even during the senate meetings. Saint Gregory's biographer, in fact, tells us that often, when the emperor would speak to the saint's father in the senate, he would be praying and not hear him. But the emperor so respected this man that he would not disturb him.

When Gregory was twenty years old he decided to become a monk, being inspired by contact with eminent monks in Constantinople, particularly Saint Theoleptos of Philadelphia. Gregory was so convinced of the value of this vocation that he persuaded his mother (his father had already died), two sisters, two brothers, and a large number of the family servants to enter monasteries.

Saint Gregory lived about ten years at Mount Athos, where he attained a good knowledge of patristic literature and a deep experience of the various problems of monastic life. He lived there a semi-eremitical form of life, in which a few monks would gather around a spiritual master. They lived, prayed, and practiced asceticism together, and on Saturdays and Sundays, went to the monastic community on which they were dependent to participate in the Liturgy and celebrate the Mysteries. This type of life greatly influenced Gregory and helped him to realize the danger of exaggerated hesychasm, which often had a contempt for liturgical life.

Around 1226, Saint Gregory left on a pilgrimage to the Holy Land and Mount Sinai. He got as far as Thessalonica, where he stayed for several years. There he joined a group of people, a kind of spiritual circle with members from various social levels, that sought to spread the practice of the Jesus Prayer outside the cloisters. They saw the prayer as a preeminent means of making the grace of baptism real and efficacious.

About 1331, Saint Gregory returned to Athos, where he decided to live in the hermitage of Saint Sabas, still keeping the balance among personal spiritual life, prayer, and liturgy. After 1338, however, his life was greatly changed when he became involved in the controversy created by Barlaam of Calabria over hesychasm.

From the time that Barlaam, a Calabrian monk, arrived in Constantinople in 1338, until the final synodal condemnation of Barlaam's followers in 1351, Saint Gregory took an active part in the controversy that struck at the very roots of hesychasm. During this period, Gregory, his supporters, and his opponents were involved in four church synods and a six-year civil war. Saint Gregory was first exonerated by a church council, then, three years later, imprisoned and excommunicated as a heretic. Finally, he was vindicated and consecrated as Archbishop of Thessalonica. The central point at issue in all this conflict was the difference between two profoundly different understandings of the spiritual life.

Barlaam had been greatly influenced by the philosophies of Neoplatonism and Nominalism (the belief that abstract ideas are mere names with no real content), and by the spirituality of Pseudo-Dionysios. He viewed humanity dualistically, seeing the spiritual life as a freeing from the body, and only the intellect as capable of contemplating God. His understanding was based on two assumptions: (1) that all knowledge, including knowledge of God, is derived from perception of sense experience (a postulate of Aristotle); and (2) that God is beyond sense experience and therefore unknowable (a postulate of neoplatonic philosophy). Barlaam believed that all knowledge of God must be indirect, passing always through objects or beings perceptible to the senses. Therefore he believed that mystical knowledge can have only an apparent reality, existing in name only, but having no reality in itself.

Barlaam was shocked by the hesychast claims that the human body could participate in prayer, that it could feel the action of divine grace, and that saints have a real vision of God. He said that the hesychasts were *omphalopsychoi* (those with the soul in the navel) and accused them of the heresy of Messalianism. (The Messalians were a sect that originated in the fourth century. They believed that, as a result of original sin, every person had a soul divided into a spiritual, angelic part, and a material, incurably demoniac part, and that the only possible means for salvation was perpetual prayer, with the aim of eliminating all passion and desire. Those who became perfect in this way claimed to experience in a knowing and feeling way the grace of God and to see God Himself.)

It is in opposition to these accusations of Barlaam that Saint Gregory wrote the *Hagiorite Tome,* which was signed in 1340–1341 by the abbots and monks of Mount Athos, and the *Triads for the Defense of the Holy Hesychasts.* Gregory gave an answer to each of Barlaam's accusations, and in doing so presented a unified theology of hesychasm.

First of all, Saint Gregory defended the close link that exists among all the components of a human being:

> But what pain or pleasure or movement is not a common activity of both body and soul?. . . There are indeed blessed passions and common activities of body and soul, which far from nailing the spirit to the flesh, serve to draw the flesh to a dignity close to that of the spirit, and persuade it too to tend towards what is above. . . . For just as the divinity of the Word of God incarnate is common to soul and body, since He has deified the flesh through the mediation of the soul to make it also accomplish the works of God; so similarly, in spiritual man, the grace of the Spirit, transmitted to the body through the soul, grants to the body also the experience of things divine, and allows it the same blessed experiences as the soul undergoes. . . . When the soul pursues this blessed activity, it deifies the body also; which, being no longer driven by corporeal and material passions . . . returns to itself and rejects all contact with evil things. Indeed, it inspires its own sanctification and inalienable divinisation, as the miracle-working relics of the saints clearly demonstrate. [22]

It was with this understanding of the unity that should be found in each human that Palamas attacked the accusation of Messalianism, which holds that evil always coexists with good in the soul. He demonstrates that this is not true by noting that a person is totally renewed by baptism, eliminating all evil, and that one only needs to live out this renewal.

Because baptism does not remove human passions and natural desires, Saint Gregory then goes on to show how these things are good, not to be eliminated but rather integrated with the spirit:

> Thus one must offer to God the passionate part of the soul, alive

and active, that it may be a living sacrifice. . . . How can this be done? Our eyes must acquire a gentle glance, attractive to others, and conveying the mercy from on high. . . . Similarly, our ears must be attentive to the divine instructions. . . . Our tongues, our hands and feet must likewise be at the service of the Divine Will. Is not such a practice of the commandments of God a common activity of body and soul, and how can such activity darken and blind the soul? [23]

Thus there is a common activity of the soul and body, and it is from this common activity that one prays and strives for ever-deeper communion with God.

For Gregory, the Jesus Prayer is the positive means to unite body and soul in prayer and to have a constant remembrance of God:

We supplicate with this continual supplication not to convince God, for he acts always spontaneously, not to draw him to us, for he is everywhere, but to lift ourselves up towards him. [24]

Because of this need for giving full attention in prayer, Saint Gregory defended the psychophysical techniques connected to the Jesus Prayer. He did not see these techniques of breathing and posture as simply mechanical ways of obtaining peace, but rather as a practical way for beginners to avoid distraction and the wandering of the mind.

Saint Gregory knew that it was of great importance to avoid distractions and to become as internally unified as possible during prayer, for, as the hesychasts knew, those who persevered in prayer could receive divine illumination. This was not simply an intellectual experience, but an illumination of the whole person. The hesychasts believed that this illumination was connected to Christ's Transfiguration on Mount Tabor:

How should he not illuminate those who commune worthily with the divine ray of his Body which is within us, lightening their souls, as he illuminated the very bodies of the disciples on Mount Tabor? For, on the day of the Transfiguration, that Body, source of the light of grace, was not yet united with our bodies; it illuminated from outside those who worthily approached it, and sent the illumination into the soul by the intermediary of the physical eyes; but now, since it is mingled with us and exists in us it illuminates the soul from within. [25]

It is, moreover, through the hesychast's use of the Jesus Prayer that this illumination occurs:

> This light at present shines in part, as a pledge, for those who through impassibility have passed beyond all that is condemned, and through pure and immaterial prayer have passed beyond all that is pure. But on the Last Day, it will deify in a manifest fashion "the sons of the Resurrection," who will rejoice in eternity and in glory in communion with Him Who has endowed our nature with a glory and splendor that is divine.[26]

Saint Gregory professed the reality of this union and of this illumination brought about through prayer. This position was opposed by Barlaam, who stated that the illumination was symbolic only, an appearance created by God. Here, as Jaroslav Pelikan explains, Gregory was faced with the paradox that is at the heart of Orthodox belief:

> The God of Christian devotion was simultaneously absolute and related, incomprehensible in his nature and yet comprehended by the saints, who participated in his nature: he was absolute by nature, related by grace.[27]

To explain how divine illumination was indeed a true union with God, Gregory made a distinction that became basic to Orthodox theology, the distinction between God's essence and His energies:

> Since one can participate in God and since the superessential essence of God is absolutely above participation, there exists something between the essence that cannot be participated in and those who participate, to make participation in God possible for them. . . . Thus, He makes himself present to all things by His manifestations and by His creative and providential energies. In one word, we must seek a God in whom we can participate in one way or another, so that by participating, each of us, in the manner proper to each, and by the analogy of participation, may receive being, life, and deification.[28]

Saint Gregory's defense was so well received by the Orthodox Church that he was called the "Light of Orthodoxy, teacher of the Church, its confirmation, ideal of monks, and invincible champion of theologians . . . preacher of grace" (Troparion of Gregory Palamas). He was canonized a mere nine years after his death, and the second Sunday of Lent was dedicated to his honor. His theology of the Jesus Prayer and hesychasm has influenced the Church's understanding of hesychasm down to our own day.

Saint Gregory's synthesis did not have a chronologically continuous influence, however, for, after 1453, the development of the Byzantine cultural and intellectual tradition was interrupted by the Turkish conquest of Byzantium. It was not until the late eighteenth century that hesychasm was to have a revival.

A MODERN REVIVAL

The hesychastic tradition did not die out in the East. Mount Athos remained the chief center of Orthodox religious life, and its libraries provided the essential patristic texts for the very few scholars of the time. In Russia, the practice of the Jesus Prayer continued to grow gradually. Saint Nil Sorsky in the fifteenth century, various monasteries in the sixteenth century, and Saint Dimitri of Rostov in the seventeenth century all advocated the use of the Jesus Prayer.

At the end of the eighteenth century, Mount Athos once again became the center for an intense diffusion of the Jesus Prayer. This was due to the work of Saint Makarios of Corinth (1731–1805) and Saint Nikodemos the Hagiorite (1748–1809). Both of these men are of great importance in the revival of hesychasm.

The Age of *The Philokalia*

During the seventeenth and eighteenth centuries, the Christian East was in a particularly deplorable condition. A number of her theologians had been trained only in Western scholastic theology and had little access to the traditional writings of the past. There were only a few isolated individuals of learning who were in a position to revive the Eastern theological, spiritual tradition.

In 1782 Nikodemos, a monk of Mount Athos, in collaboration with Makarios, the Bishop of Corinth, published at Venice an anthology of patristic texts by authors from the fourth to the fifteenth centuries, which was called *The Philokalia of Neptic Saints. The Philokalia* (the Greek meaning "love of beauty") deals chiefly with the theory and practice of prayer, especially the Jesus Prayer. This book became the source for a revival of hesychasm in the nineteenth century in both Greece and Russia, where the book was translated into both Slavonic and Russian.

The Philokalia was to have a special influence in Russia. In 1793, the renowned elder Saint Paisius Velichkovsky (1722–1794), a Ukrainian, published at Saint Petersburg a Slavonic edition of *The Philokalia,* called the *Dobrotolubiye* ("The Love of the Good"). Saint Paisius was a monk of Mount Athos, where he founded a Russian monastery; he later went to Romania and became Abbot of the Monastery of Niamets. Through his guidance this monastery became a center for the translation of the Greek Fathers into Slavonic.

There Saint Paisius placed great emphasis on the continual practice of the Jesus Prayer, and it was through his influence that many monasteries were introduced to hesychasm.

In the *Dobrotolubiye,* Saint Paisius, who had already translated various Greek texts into Slavonic, did not merely translate the texts printed in the Greek *Philokalia,* but added other original texts as well. His completed work was widely circulated in Russia and was used by monks and lay people alike. This is seen, for example, in the work *The Way of the Pilgrim,* where the pilgrim, a layman, buys a copy for two rubles.

Nineteenth-Century Russia

Nineteenth-century Russia became a great center for the practice of the Jesus Prayer. This renewal had at its heart certain significant personalities, particularly the line of *startzy* (elders) at Optino and the solitary personality of the greatest saint of the contemporary Russian Church, Saint Seraphim of Sarov.

Optino was a sixteenth-century hermitage near the little town of Kozelsk in central Russia. At the end of the eighteenth century, when the hermitage was nearly abandoned, the Metropolitan of Moscow asked a disciple of Saint Paisius, the Archimandrite Makarios, to send a small group of monks to reestablish the hermitage. They did this in 1821, and soon the elders of Optino acquired unique fame throughout all Russia.

These elders were sought after by people from all levels of society and all walks of life. In the elders' eyes, the senator, the poor peasant, the student all seemed equally suffering and in need of spiritual medicine. Prominent literary figures such as Gogol, Dostoevsky, Khomiakov, Soloviev, and Leo Tolstoy came seeking direction. The Optino *startzy* exercised a prophetic ministry, and to all who came, they taught the value of the Jesus Prayer.

The other bright light of nineteenth-century hesychasm was Saint Seraphim of Sarov (1759–1833). He entered the monastery of Sarov at the age of nineteen, spending his first fifteen years in community life and then thirty years in seclusion. He used his years of seclusion as his training for the office of elder, and in 1825, opened the doors of his cell to all who would come to him. Saint Seraphim constantly prayed the Jesus Prayer, and, in the tradition of Saint Symeon the New Theologian and Saint Gregory Palamas, was granted the vision of the Divine and Uncreated Light. In Seraphim's case the Divine Light actually took a visible form, outwardly transforming his body.

The hesychast tradition manifested itself in Russia in the nineteenth century on many different cultural levels and in very different forms, among laity and clergy alike. Saint Ignatius Brianchaninov (1807–1867), Bishop of Kostroma, besides writing on the value of the Jesus Prayer for all people, published a more complete Slavonic edition of the *Dobrotolubiye,* and Saint Theophan the Recluse (1815–1894), another important teacher of the Jesus Prayer, prepared a greatly expanded translation of the *Philokalia* in five volumes—not in Slavonic, but in the Russian vernacular.

In addition to these learned works on the Jesus Prayer, there appeared at the same time a simple story of a wanderer, called *The Sincere Tales of a Pilgrim to His Spiritual Father,* or *The Way of the Pilgrim.* It is the story of a simple Russian peasant who becomes a pilgrim, a wanderer traveling back and forth across Russia. He is in search of a way to pray without ceasing and discovers this in the Jesus Prayer. He buys a copy of the *Dobrotolubiye* and frequently consults it to explain both the Jesus Prayer itself and the importance of this prayer for the whole of the Christian life.

The story takes place sometime between the Crimean War (1855) and the abolition of Russian serfdom (1861). Its first edition appeared in 1884 at Kazan and stated that the work was printed according to a manuscript obtained from a monk of Mount Athos. The second part was published in 1911 in Moscow.

There is some controversy over whether these are actual autobio-graphical tales or simply spiritual novels. Whichever they are, these works have had a tremendous impact in popularizing the practice of the Jesus Prayer. The pilgrim recommends the prayer to all Christians, in the words of Saint Gregory Palamas:

> Not only should we ourselves, in accordance with God's will, pray unceasingly in the Name of Jesus Christ, but we are bound to reveal it and teach it to others, to everyone in general, religious and secular, learned and simple, men, women, and children, and to inspire them all to prayer without ceasing.[29]

The Twentieth-Century West

In the present-day Western world the Jesus Prayer is becoming more widely known and practiced, as it has been for centuries in the Christian East. This is due in part to the immigration of Orthodox Christians to the West, especially Russian and other Slavic immigrants.

There have also been new editions and translations made of *The Philokalia* and other older writings on the Jesus Prayer. In English, a partial, but uncritical, translation from the Russian *Dobrotolubiye* in two volumes by E. Kadloubovsky and G. Palmer was first published in 1951 and 1954. The same translators also produced a collection of various texts on the Jesus Prayer, compiled by Chariton of Valamo in Finland in the first half of this century. This contains principally texts by Theophan the Recluse and Ignatius Brianchaninov and is titled in English, *The Art of Prayer*. In 1930, R. M. French published an English translation of the Russian work *The Way of the Pilgrim,* which has been issued in several successive editions. Other new translations of *The Way of the Pilgrim* have also been published more recently. Since 1979 Bishop Kallistos Ware, G. E. H. Palmer, and Philip Sherrard have issued four of five promised volumes of the complete translation of *The Philokalia* from the Greek. This promises to be a boon for greater understanding of the Jesus Prayer among English-speaking Orthodox Christians. Finally, many collections of sayings from *The Philiokalia* have been published, and other new works about the Jesus Prayer have been written.

RECEIVING THE GIFT

The Jesus Prayer is a great gift which comes to us from our Fathers throughout the centuries, but, like any gift, it must be opened and used to be really appreciated. It is a rich part of our Eastern Christian heritage and has led to the sanctification and illumination of many, opening them more fully to the active and energetic presence of the Holy Spirit.

This gift is given not only to the Church as a whole but to you personally, under the guidance of your spiritual father, to be used, to be prayed, to become a part of life. Under the guidance of your spiritual father, you will learn how you should pray the Jesus Prayer. The prayer may be used at assigned times in the day, or it may be used in times of quiet, particularly when you are involved in some activity that frees you from talk and provides a time of quiet. This may be some repetitive activity in the home, or it may be when you are driving, particularly when the traffic is not causing inner turmoil. The prayer can fill your heart when you are being kept on hold on the telephone, or while waiting in some office for an appointment. The prayer may be prayed when you wake up in the morning, or before going to bed. You may even want to wake up in the night and pray it in the quiet of dark silence.

The only way that this can happen is for you to take to heart the words of our Fathers and begin gradually to repeat these words to yourself, to let the prayer become a part of you, like the beating of your heart or the breath of your lungs. Then you can share in this gift, and thus attain a more constant recollection of God and openness to His presence, to whom be glory, honor, and praise, Father, Son, and Holy Spirit, now and ever and unto ages of ages. Amen.

ENDNOTES

1   Chariton of Valamo, compiler, *The Art of Prayer,* E. Kadloubovsky and G. Palmer, trans. (London: Faber and Faber Ltd., 1966), p. 267.

2   A Monk of the Eastern Church, *The Prayer of Jesus* (New York: Desclee Co., 1967), p. 11.

3   *Ibid.,* p. 16.

4   Benedicta Ward, trans., *The Sayings of the Desert Fathers* (Oxford: A. R. Mowbray and Company, 1975), p. 111.

5   Pseudo-Makarios, *Fifty Spiritual Homilies,* XV, 20, George Maloney, trans. (New York, Paulist Press, 1992), pp. 115–116.

6   Evagrios, *Chapters on Prayer,* 9, 11, 66, 110, as found in *Evagrius Ponticus,* John Eudes Bamberger, trans. (Kalamazoo: Cistercian Publications, 1978), pp. 57, 66, 73.

7   John Meyendorff, *St. Gregory Palamas and Orthodox Spirituality* (Crestwood, NY: St. Vladimir's Seminary Press, 1974), p. 18.

8   Diadochos of Photike, *One Hundred Chapters on Perfection,* 85, as found in *The Philokalia,* vol. I, Palmer, Sherrard, Ware, trans. (London: Faber and Faber, 1979), p. 285.

9   *Ibid.,* 59, p. 270.

10 Philemon, *A Discourse on Abba Philemon,* as found in *The Philokalia,* vol. II, Palmer, Sherrard, Ware, trans. (London: Faber and Faber, 1981), p. 347.

11 *Ibid.,* p. 348.

12 John Klimakos, *The Ladder of Divine Ascent,* Steps 28 and 27, Luibheid and Russell, trans. (New York: Paulist Press, 1982), pp. 275, 263, 269–270.

13 Pseudo-Hesychios, *On Watchfulness and Prayer,* 196, as found in *The Philokalia,* vol. I, p. 197.

14 Maximos the Confessor, *Ambigua, Patrologia Greca,* vol. 91, 1076 b and c. Translation found in Meyendorff, *op. cit.,* pp. 44–45.

15 Jaroslav Pelikan, *The Spirit of Eastern Christendom* (600–1700) (Chicago: University of Chicago Press, 1974), pp. 255, 257.

16 Symeon the New Theologian, *The Discourses,* XXXVI, 9–10, de Catanzaro, trans. (New York: Paulist Press, 1980), pp. 373–375.

17 Nicetas cites here a passage from Symeon's *Discourses, Ibid.,* pp. 200–201.

18 Monk of the Eastern Church, *op. cit.,* p. 46.

19 Gregory of Sinai, *On Contemplative Life and Prayer,* 1, 3, as found in Meyendorff, *op. cit.,* pp. 68–70.

20 Nikephoros, *On Guarding the Heart,* conclusion, as found in *The Philokalia,* vol. IV, Palmer, Sherrard, Ware, trans. (London: Faber and Faber, 1995), pp. 205–206.

21 Monk of the Eastern Church, *op. cit.,* p. 39.

22 Palamas, *Triads,* II, 2, 12 as found in Nicholas Gendle, trans., *Gregory Palamas, The Triads* (New York: Paulist Press, 1983), pp. 51–52.

23 Palamas, *Triads,* 2, 20, *ibid.,* p. 55.

24 Palamas, *Triads,* II, 1, 30 as found in John Meyendorff, *A Study of Gregory Palamas* (New York: St. Vladimir's Seminary Press, 1998), p. 141.
25 Palamas, *Triads,* I, 3, 38, *ibid.,* p. 151.
26 Palamas, *Triads,* II, 3, 66 as found in Gendle, trans, *op. cit.,* p. 67.
27 Pelikan, *op. cit.,* p. 268.
28 Palamas, *Triads,* III, 2, 24 as found in Meyendorff, *St. Gregory Palamas and Orthodox Spirituality,* pp. 123, 125.
29 R. M. French, trans., *The Way of the Pilgrim* and *The Pilgrim Continues His Way* (New York: Ballantine Books, 1974), p. 41.